It's me... a Frog

Om KIDZ
An imprint of Om Books International

First Published in 2019 by

Om Kidz | Om Books International

Corporate & Editorial Office
A-12, Sector 64, Noida 201 301
Uttar Pradesh, India
Phone: +91 120 477 4100
Email: editorial@ombooks.com
Website: www.ombooksinternational.com

Sales Office
107, Ansari Road, Darya Ganj
New Delhi 110 002, India
Phone: +91 11 4000 9000
Email: sales@ombooks.com
Website: www.ombooks.com

ISBN: 978-93-86410-38-2

Printed in India

10 9 8 7 6 5 4 3 2 1

Contents

WHO ARE YOU?

Scientific Name

Rana temporaria

of Common Frog

Hello! I am a frog. I belong to the Anura family of tailless amphibians.

WHAT DO YOU LOOK LIKE?

We have bulging eyes and smooth, moist skin. We also have strong, webbed feet which help us leap and swim.

Poisonous Skin Glands

Many frog species have poisonous skin glands. The Golden Poison Dart frog is known as one of the most poisonous creatures on Earth.

WHAT DO YOU EAT?

We feed mainly on insects, worms, bugs, rodents and mites. However, some species also eat other frogs and small reptiles.

DO YOU HAVE TEETH?

Yes. We have very small cone-like teeth in our upper jaw. Usually, we also have vomerine teeth on the roof of our mouth. Most of us have a toothless lower jaw.

Gunther's Marsupial Frogs

Gunther's marsupial frogs are the only known species of frogs to have teeth in their lower jaws.

WHERE DO YOU LIVE?

Bright and Colourful

Tropical frogs have bright and colourful skin.

Aquatic - found in or near water

A new word to learn

Army of Frogs

A group of frogs is known as an 'army'.

WHO ALL ARE THERE IN YOUR FAMILY?

My family consists of over 4700 species of frogs. We belong to the Anura family. We are found on every continent, except Antarctica.

WHO ARE YOUR PREDATORS?

A new word to learn

Camouflage - the natural colour of an animal that makes it look like its surroundings

Poisonous Skin

Some frogs have skin that secretes poison to protect them from their enemies. Certain species of frogs also use **camouflage** to escape from enemies.

We have several predators, including snakes, birds, sharp-toothed fish, water shrews and several small animals, such as hedgehogs.

DO YOU LAY EGGS?

Yes. The eggs vary from a few hundred to several thousands.

The eggs then float on water in clusters. Breeding mostly takes place in fresh water.

Baby Frogs

Baby frogs are called tadpoles or froglets.

WHAT IS THE DIFFERENCE BETWEEN A FROG AND A TOAD?

Lower, football-shaped eyes
Mostly lives on land
Can run or hop
Short legs
Toad
Lays eggs in a chain
Thick and dry skin
Stout Body

HOW DO YOU DRINK WATER?

We don't use our mouth to drink water. We absorb water through our **permeable** skin.

A new word to learn

permeable - allowing liquid or gases to pass through

HOW DO YOU CATCH YOUR PREY?

We use our super-sticky tongue to catch our prey. The adhesive force of our tongue is 50% higher than our body mass.

HOW DO YOU COMMUNICATE?

We croak! Every frog species has its own unique call, which they use to communicate with each other. The croaks of some frog species can be heard from a distance of almost 1.5 km.

HOW FAR CAN YOU JUMP?

Many of us can jump around 20 times our body length. However, there are some frog species which can only hop short distances because they have short legs.

WHO ARE GLASS FROGS?

Glass frogs are beautiful creatures with transparent skin. They are also known as leaf frogs. These frogs live near trees and plants.

Nocturnal Creatures

Glass frogs are active only at night. Hence, it is difficult for predators to spot them.

WHO ARE POISON DART FROGS?

Poison Dart frogs are considered some of the most toxic creatures on Earth. These frogs are quite colourful. Their skin can be of vibrant shades of yellow, blue, green, orange and red.

Warning Signals

The vibrant colours of Poison Dart frogs indicate how toxic they are. Their colourful skin serves as a warning to predators that these frogs are poisonous.

WHO ARE FLYING FROGS?

Flying frogs are tree-dwelling creatures. They can jump 9 to 15 m with the help of the expanded webbing between their fingers and toes.

Special Features

Flying frogs have a broad heads with a round snout, huge eyes and eardrums. They have a slender body and long legs.

WHO ARE HYLID TREE FROGS?

Hylids are slender and long-legged tree-dwelling creatures. They are around 4 inches long and have adhesive disks on the tips of their toes and fingers. These disks help them climb. These frogs belong to the Hylidae family.

Jewel-like Eyes

Hylids often have jewel-like eyes which gleam with flecks of copper or gold. Their shiny skin varies widely in colour and usually has a metallic sheen to it.

ACTIVITY TIME

FROG ORIGAMI

Things You'll Need

- Green craft paper
- Googly eyes
- Glue bottle

Take a square-shaped green craft paper and fold it into a triangle. Fold it once again to make the triangle half its size. Then, unfold this part.

Fold the two bottom corners inwards so that they meet at the centre of the bottom edge. Now, turn the paper over.

03

Fold the edges in such a way that they meet in the middle. Let the corners extend out from behind.

Next, fold the bottom edge upwards. Fold it twice over. Fold the corners to make the frog's feet.

04

Paste the googly eyes.

05

Voilà! Your origami frog is ready!

The frog is hungry! Help it reach the yummy flies.